INFORMATION
EXPLORER
JUNIOR

Citing Sources: Learning to Use the Copyright Page

The intellectual property of this book was created . . . → by Suzy Rabbat

CHERRY LAKE PUBLISHING · ANN ARBOR, MICHIGAN

A NOTE TO PARENTS AND TEACHERS: Please remind your children how to stay safe online before they do the activities in this book.

CHERRY LAKE Publishing

A NOTE TO KIDS: Always remember your safety comes first!

Published in the United States of America
by Cherry Lake Publishing
Ann Arbor, Michigan
www.cherrylakepublishing.com

Content Adviser: Gail Dickinson, PhD, Associate Professor,
Old Dominion University, Norfolk, Virginia

Photo Credits: Cover, ©Aletia/Shutterstock, Inc.; page 5, ©Lisa F. Young/Shutterstock,
Inc.; page 6, ©Digitalpress/Dreamstime.com; page 8, ©Canettistock/Dreamstime.com;
page 15, ©gasa/Shutterstock, Inc.; page 21, ©wow/Shutterstock, Inc.

Library of Congress Cataloging-in-Publication Data
Rabbat, Suzy.
  Citing sources : learning to use the copyright page / by Suzy Rabbat.
     pages cm — (Information explorer junior)
  Includes bibliographical references and index.
  ISBN 978-1-62431-023-2 (lib. bdg.) — ISBN 978-1-62431-047-8 (pbk.) —
ISBN 978-1-62431-071-3 (e-book)
  1. Bibliographical citations—Juvenile literature. 2. Copyright—Juvenile literature.
I. Title.
  PN171.F56R33 2013
  346.04'82—dc23   2012035763

Cherry Lake Publishing would like to acknowledge the work of The Partnership for
21st Century Skills. Please visit *www.21stcenturyskills.org* for more information.

Printed in the United States of America
Corporate Graphics Inc.
January 2013
CLSP12

Table of Contents

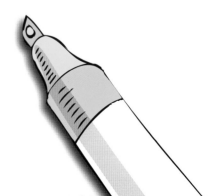

CHAPTER ONE

All Kinds of Property

The book you're looking at now is someone's **property**. It may belong to your school library. That makes it the school's property. Maybe you borrowed it from the public library. In that case, the public library owns the book. It's the library's property.

What are some things that belong to you? Your video games, books, and clothes are all examples. These are your property. They are all things that you can see and touch. But there's another kind of property. Let's take a look.

Nate loves playing video games. One of the games he owns is called *Amazing Soccer*. A video game designer named Jenny Smith

Video games are just one of many types of intellectual property.

developed this game. Jenny designed how *Amazing Soccer* would look. She also decided how Nate and other kids would play soccer with the game. Jenny Smith was the creator of the **intellectual property**. Her thoughts and ideas were used to create the game.

If you've ever written a song, you have created intellectual property.

The word **intellect** has to do with a person's mind. It refers to someone's thoughts or ideas. When someone writes a song, the words and melody are created by the songwriter. The songwriter is the creator of this intellectual property. A drawing is an artist's intellectual property. The artist is the one who imagined the drawing and then sketched it. The sketch is the intellectual property created by the artist.

Activity

Who created the intellectual property for this book? Whose ideas and thoughts went into writing it? Hint: You'll find the answer on the title page.

CHAPTER TWO

What Is Copyright?

Nate's friend Mike lives down the block. Mike just got a new bike. He left the bike on his driveway when he went inside for lunch. Nate would love to try out Mike's new bike.

A person's bike is his or her property.

Would this be a good time to borrow it? Mike's not using it. Nate could get it back before Mike finishes his lunch.

Something doesn't seem right. Nate can't borrow Mike's bike without asking. Why? It is Mike's property. Nate should ask for permission first. The same is true about using someone's ideas or intellectual property.

The United States has a law called **copyright**. This protects the creative work of authors, designers, and artists. The copyright law says people cannot use another person's work without the owner's permission. The copyright symbol is ©. This symbol tells who owns the intellectual property. Books include their copyright information on a page at the front. In this book, it is on page 2. You can find the same information on video games, CDs, DVDs, and other products.

Sometimes, intellectual property belongs to a group or a company. Game designer Jenny Smith works for a company called Video Fun. Video Fun makes and sells *Amazing Soccer*. Video Fun is the game's intellectual property owner. The copyright symbol appears with the company's name.

The copyright symbol appears by the name of the intellectual property owner.

To get a copy of this activity, visit www.cherrylakepublishing.com/activities.

Activity

Turn to page 2 in this book. Can you find the copyright symbol? What is the name of the publishing company that owns the copyright for this book? Other products have things similar to a book's copyright page. Pick up a video game or a DVD. Look for the copyright symbol. It is usually on the disc. You can also find it on the case or box that came with it. Can you find who owns the intellectual property of each item?

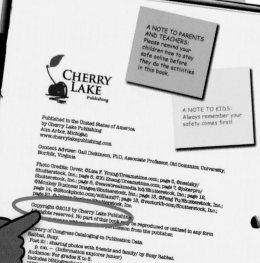

CHAPTER THREE

Smart Steps to Using Information

Kids often use books and Web sites to find facts for school projects. They take notes to remember important ideas. Remember, the information in books and Web sites is someone's intellectual property. You need to be responsible about using them. Follow these steps:

1. Read the book or Web site carefully. Try reading a few sentences or a paragraph at a time. Stop and ask yourself these questions:
   - What is the author's message?
   - How can I explain the idea in my own words without changing the meaning?

Paraphrasing puts ideas into your own words.

2. Write your notes in your own words. This is called **paraphrasing**. This is not just copying down phrases or sentences. Paraphrasing rewords ideas in a way that makes sense to you. It shows that you really understood what you read. Later, you can organize your facts in a way that is all your own.

To get a copy of this activity, visit www.cherrylakepublishing.com/activities.

Activity

Here's a page from a book called *All About Bats*. Can you paraphrase this information? Use a dictionary to help you understand any words you do not know.

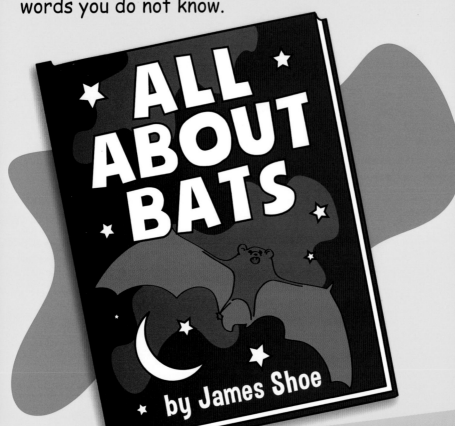

ALL ABOUT BATS

by James Shoe

continued on page 15 →

Big brown bats are covered with glossy, copper-colored fur. They have small ears and a broad nose. These nocturnal creatures cruise the sky, scooping up flying insects such as moths and mosquitoes for their dinner.

Big Brown Bat
- body covered with reddish-brown fur
- small ears, wide nose
- sleeps during the day, awake at night
- eats flying insects
- catches insects while it flies

3. Write down the author's first and last names. Include the book or Web site's title, too. In a book, this information is on the copyright or title page. For a Web site, it's usually on the home page. Writing this down will help you credit your sources later.

Remember to write down information about all the sources you use as you take notes.

Carefully note the URLs of any Web site where you find information you plan to use.

4. Note the page number or Web address where you found facts and ideas. The Web address is sometimes called the Universal Resource Locator, or URL. It is found at the top of a Web page. It usually starts with *www*. Some URLs can be very long. Just record the address up to the forward slash, or /.

CHAPTER FOUR

Giving Credit

You should always show where you found the information you used in a project. Do this by creating a **citation**. A citation is a list of facts that tell about the book or Web site you used.

Here's what you need to write a citation for a book:

1. Author's name
2. Title of the book
3. Page number(s) where you found facts or ideas. This is helpful if you or anyone reading your report wants to check your facts.

When you write a citation, separate the different parts using commas. This is a citation for the book on bats:

James Shoe, All About Bats, p. 23

Do you need to write a citation for a Web site? Here's what to include:

1. Author's name. Often this is found on the bottom of the home page.
2. Web site title. Not all Web sites have a title. If you can't find one, skip this step.
3. Web site URL
4. Date you viewed the Web site. The Internet is constantly changing. It's a good idea to include this information in case the Web page is changed or removed.

A Web site citation may look like this:

Emma Wilson, The Brown Bat, www.brownbats.org, November 18, 2012

Activity

Can you make citations for these sources?

Book

Title: *A Day at the Park*

Author: Peggy Wood

Page number: 17

Web site

URL: www.shipatsea.net

Author: Edward West

Title: Seeing Ships at Sea

Date viewed: April 14, 2013

Hint for citing a book:
Author, title, page number

Hint for citing a Web site:
Author, title, URL, date

Information and ideas are all around us. They're in books, magazines, pictures, videos, and on the Internet. Be a responsible user of information. Here's how:

- Use your own words to show what you understand.
- Use a citation to show where you found your information.

Respect the intellectual property of others!

How will you respect intellectual property?

Glossary

citation (sye-TAY-shuhn) a statement that shows where someone found information

copyright (KAH-pee-rite) the legal right to control the use of something created, such as a song or a book

intellect (IN-tuh-lekt) the power of the mind to think, reason, understand, learn, and create

intellectual property (in-tuh-LEK-choo-uhl PRAH-pur-tee) creative works that are legally protected by copyright, trademark, or patent

paraphrasing (PAR-uh-fraze-ing) saying or writing something in a different way than the original without changing the meaning

property (PRAH-pur-tee) anything that is owned by an individual, group, or company

Find Out More

BOOK

Berg, Brook. *When Marion Copied: Learning About Plagiarism*. Madison, WI: Upstart Books, 2006.

Throp, Claire. *Put It Together: Using Information*. Chicago: Heinemann Library, 2010.

WEB SITE

Cyberbee Copyright

www.cyberbee.com/cb_copyright.swf

Use this interactive tool to learn more about copyright and the responsible use of information.

Kentucky Virtual Library Presents: How to Do Research

www.kyvl.org/kids/f_homebase.html

This site is full of tips and tricks about finding and using information.

Index

About the Author

Suzy Rabbat is a national board certified school librarian who works as a school library consultant. She lives in the northwestern suburbs of Chicago.